The University of North Carolina

Social Study Series

INCOME AND WAGES IN THE SOUTH

THE UNIVERSITY OF NORTH CAROLINA
SOCIAL STUDY SERIES

Published in coöperation with the Institute for Research in Social Science under the general editorship of Howard W. Odum

Odum and Johnson: *The Negro and His Songs*..................$3.00
Puckett: *Folk Beliefs of the Southern Negro*.................... 5.00
Odum and Johnson: *Negro Workaday Songs*.................... 3.00
Odum and others: *Southern Pioneers*............................ 2.00
Pound: *Law and Morals*.. 2.00
Giddings: *The Scientific Study of Human Society*................ 2.00
Odum and Willard: *Systems of Public Welfare*.................. 2.00
Branson: *Farm Life Abroad*................................... 2.00
Ross: *Roads to Social Peace*.................................. 1.50
Willey: *The Country Newspaper*................................ 1.50
Jordan: *Children's Interests in Reading*....................... 1.50
Odum: *Public Welfare and Social Work*......................... 1.50
North: *Social Differentiation*................................. 2.50
Knight: *Among the Danes*..................................... 2.50
Steiner and Brown: *The North Carolina Chain Gang*............ 2.00
Lou: *Juvenile Courts in the United States*...................... 3.00
Carter: *The Social Theories of L. T. Hobhouse*................. 1.50
Brown: *A State Movement in Railroad Development*............. 5.00
Miller: *Town and Country*..................................... 2.00
Mitchell: *William Gregg: Factory Master of the Old South*...... 3.00
Metfessel: *Phonophotography in Folk Music*.................... 3.00
Wager: *County Government in North Carolina*.................. 5.00
Brown: *Public Poor Relief in North Carolina*................... 2.00
Walker: *Social Work and the Training of Social Workers*........ 2.00
Herring: *Welfare Work in Mill Villages*........................ 5.00
Vance: *Human Factors in Cotton Culture*....................... 3.00
Johnson: *John Henry*.. 2.00
Rhyne: *Some Southern Cotton Mill Workers and Their Villages*.. 2.50

The University of North Carolina Press
Chapel Hill, N. C.

The Baker and Taylor Co.
New York

Oxford University Press
London

Maruzen-Kabushiki-Kaisha
Tokyo

INCOME AND WAGES IN THE SOUTH

BY

CLARENCE HEER

Research Associate in the Institute for Research in Social Science in the University of North Carolina

CHAPEL HILL

THE UNIVERSITY OF NORTH CAROLINA PRESS

1930

PREFACE

THIS preliminary study of wages and income in the South grew out of the immediate need for comparative data which arose in connection with regional studies of economic and social situations now being made by the Institute for Research in Social Science at the University of North Carolina. The study owes its publication in its present form to the timeliness of the subject and to the current demand for information in the field covered. These factors have been allowed to outweigh the advantages of making a more exhaustive study or one which incorporated the new census data, either of which courses would have involved delay.

Although the author assumes full responsibility for the statistical data and for the conclusions drawn therefrom, the study, nevertheless, owes much to coöperative effort. Special thanks are due Dean D. D. Carroll and Professor Howard W. Odum, of the Board of Governors, for making possible a preliminary inquiry at this time. The author is under especial obligation to Miss Harriet L. Herring, Research Associate, who not only contributed valuable ideas and sound criticism, but generously gave the author the benefit both of her extensive researches in the field of southern industry and of her first-hand knowledge of the South. He is under especial obligation, also, to Miss Katharine Jocher, Assistant Director of the Institute, who prepared the manuscript for the press.

Finally, the author wishes to acknowledge his indebtedness to his wife for her substantial assistance in the tedious work of compiling the statistical data and for many suggestions and criticisms.

C. H.

Chapel Hill, N. C.
April, 1930.

CONTENTS

INCOME AND WAGES IN THE SOUTH

CHAPTER I

THE INCOME STATUS OF THE SOUTH

GEOGRAPHICAL regions, like individuals, may be classified on the basis of their income status. In some parts of the country, the average level of income per inhabitant is high. This may be due to the presence of a relatively large number of wealthy persons or to the fact that salary and wage scales are higher than elsewhere. In other parts of the country, the level of income is low. This condition is usually found to exist where there are few persons of great wealth, where the bulk of the population is engaged in unproductive employments, and where salaries and wages are lower than elsewhere.

Although regional differences in the average level of money incomes bear no necessary relation to the quality of life which the various regions afford, it is none the less essential that such differences be carefully analyzed and measured. In a pecuniary society, whose economic ramifications extend over an ever widening area, differences in income levels may have important practical consequences. They may cause entire industries to change their location or may set in motion a tide of migration. They may be responsible for inequalities in taxation, for differences in the purchasing habits of consumers and, not infrequently, for sectional conflicts of interest and outlook.

Incomes and wages in the South have been considerably below the average obtaining in the rest of the country for upwards of sixty years. Until comparatively recently, the effects of this condition were mainly local and excited little outside attention. This is no longer the case. The new industry of the South is part and parcel of a larger economy, and the comparative level of southern wages has accordingly become a matter of nation-wide concern.

Since it is in the field of industry that the new forces at work in the South have been most widely felt, it is not strange that the interest of industrial enterprisers, labor leaders, and students of economics has been centered chiefly upon the wages of southern factory workers. Wages and incomes in the various gainful employments are, however, to a considerable degree interdependent. In the South, as elsewhere, the earnings of factory workers are affected by the rewards offered in other occupations, and by prevailing income standards. The problem of industrial wages in the South is thus inextricably bound up with a much larger problem, that of discovering the various factors which make the general average of southern income what it is today. Incomes in the South are quite generally lower than in the rest of the United States. This generalization holds whether the incomes under comparison be those of farmers, ministers, teachers, skilled trade unionists, unorganized common laborers, employees of strictly private enterprises, employees of railroads and other public utilities, or servants of the state.

It is the purpose of the following study to measure and to analyze these income differentials. More specifically it is proposed to compare the general level of income in the South with that of the rest of the country and to observe the variations in the income and wage differentials applicable to particular occupations and employments. It is also proposed to inquire into the nature of some of the factors which are responsible for the income disparity between the South and elsewhere and to consider what influences, if any, are at work to remove them.

To carry out these proposals in any adequate fashion would require the development of much new information and an amount of original research far beyond the powers of any single investigator. This basic work still remains to be done; the present study offers no substitute for the deficiency. Its purpose is merely to gather together such fragmentary statistics on income in the South as now exist ready at hand and to suggest tentative answers to the questions raised on the basis of the uncertain light afforded by data which are admittedly incomplete and imperfect.

THE SOUTH AND ITS CHARACTERISTICS

The term "South" as currently used has no definite connotation. Roughly speaking, it means the southeastern portion of the United States, but just how far west and north its domain extends is a question over which there might be disagreement. It is necessary, however, to draw a line somewhere, and, for the purpose of the present study, it has been drawn at Texas and Oklahoma in the west, and at Missouri, Kentucky, West Virginia, and Maryland in the north. As thus delimited, the South comprises ten states, Virginia, North Carolina, South Carolina, Georgia, Florida, Tennessee, Alabama, Mississippi, Arkansas, and Louisiana.

The question at once arises as to whether these southern states possess any characteristics, other than geographical propinquity and a common historical background, which justify their being lumped together for the purpose of an income study. It is a common impression that the South is rapidly becoming industrialized. In this respect, at least, the southern states are by no means all alike. If it is proper to measure the rate of industrialization of a state by the percentage increase in the number of its factory wage earners, then five of the states under consideration possessed the distinction of leading the entire country with respect to the rapidity of their industrial growth during the period from 1919 to 1927. In South Carolina, according to the Census of Manufactures, the number of wage earners in manufacturing establishments increased by 37 per cent during the eight years in question. North Carolina came next with an increase of 30 per cent, followed by Georgia with an increase of 25 per cent, Tennessee with an increase of 21 per cent, and Alabama with an increase of 11 per cent. In the remaining southern states, on the other hand, the number of industrial workers showed slight declines.

It would be a mistake, however, to attach too much importance to industry in characterizing the South. Most of the region's recent industrial progress has been due to the expansion of a single activity, the manufacture of textiles. Even in the most industrialized of the southern states, the proportion of the total working population engaged in manufacturing is considerably below the proportion found in the industrial states of the Northeast. The distinguishing characteristic, which all of the southern states have in common, is the fact that they are still predominantly rural and agricultural. Six of them appear among the ten states which, in 1920, had the lowest ratios of urban to rural population in the entire country. Seven of them are to be found among the ten states which outranked the entire country with respect to the relative size of their farm populations in 1925. North Carolina has a higher proportion of factory wage earners than any state in the South. Nevertheless, over half of its population lived on farms in 1925.

Aside from the predominance of agriculture, another characteristic which distinguishes practically all of the southern states is the prevalence of farm tenancy. Of the ten states which, in 1925, led the entire country with respect to the proportion of tenant-operated farms, no less than seven belonged to the South. All of the southern states are of course alike in having a larger proportion of Negroes than any other states in the union. In 1920, the ratio of Negroes to the total population ranged from 19 per cent in Tennessee to 52 per cent in Mississippi.

A final common characteristic of the southern states is their low average of wealth. Here again they stand out sharply from the rest of the country. Thus, a ranking of all the states of the union on the basis of per capita tangible wealth, as estimated by the Bureau of the Census for 1922, shows eight of the ten poorest states to be southern. This fact alone would seem to offer sufficient warrant for treating the South as a unit for the purpose of the present study.

STATISTICAL SOURCES

Existing statistical materials bearing on the relative level of income in the South fall roughly into four general classes. Some light on the subject may be obtained from federal income tax statistics. A second source of information is the excellent study of the National Bureau of Economic Research entitled *Income in the Various States,*[1] which contains an estimated allocation by states of the national income totals for the years 1919 to 1921 inclusive. The various

[1] Leven, *Income in the Various States,* National Bureau of Economic Research, New York, 1925.

publications of the Bureau of the Census and of other federal agencies such as the Department of Agriculture, the Interstate Commerce Commission, and the Bureau of Education, offer a wealth of information, segregated by states, concerning total values produced, number of workers employed, and aggregate salary and wage payments in specific lines of economic activity. Finally, there are at hand a number of studies, made for the most part by the Department of Labor, which afford geographical comparisons of the hourly wage rates paid in specific trades and occupations. The evidence obtainable from each of these sources will be considered in turn.

FEDERAL INCOME TAX RETURNS

When it is realized that fewer than 10 per cent of the gainfully employed of the country file federal income tax returns, it will be seen at once that these returns offer very little help to the investigator interested in measuring geographical differences in the general income level. Practically all that the returns tell us is the number of single persons and heads of families whose individual or family incomes fall above certain variable limits. Even this information is not supplied completely. Concerning the incomes received by the 90 per cent of the gainfully employed who do not file returns, the tax statistics are silent.

In spite of the above considerations, it is probably legitimate for the purpose in view to attach some significance to the ratio which the number of persons filing returns in each state bears to the total state population. Table I sets forth such state ratios for the calendar year 1926. If indicative of nothing else, this table is useful as showing the variations from state to state in the proportion of the total population which has attained or has surpassed a reasonably adequate income standard. It will be seen that the proportion of persons with incomes large enough to require the filing of returns is only about one-third as great in the South as in the rest of the country. Moreover, of the ten states having the lowest percentage of income taxpayers, no less than eight belong to the southern group under consideration.

ESTIMATED INCOME PER CAPITA

More revealing evidence of the difference in income levels as between the South and the rest of the country is furnished by the National Bureau of Economic Research estimates of aggregate income by states. Table II gives a comparison, based on these estimates, of the average per capita income of the South and the corresponding average for the remainder of the country with respect to the only years for which such data are available, viz., 1919 to 1921. It will be seen from this table that the per capita income of the South fell short of the comparable figure for the rest of the country by 45 per cent in 1919, 54 per cent in 1920, and 58 per cent in 1921. In other words, during the years in question Southerners were obliged to get along on an average income less than half as great as the average income received by residents of other sections of the United States.

The shortcomings of the figures presented in Table II are obvious. In the first place they are ten years old. In the second place general averages, obtained by dividing the aggregate of incomes received from all sources by the total population, can have but limited significance. No infor-

TABLE I

Percentage of Total Population Filing Federal Income Tax Returns for Calendar Year 1926.

Rank	State	Percentage of Population Filing Returns	Rank	State	Percentage of Population Filing Returns
1	California	7.31	25	Vermont	2.45
2	New York	6.66	26	Minnesota	2.42
3	Nevada	6.20	27	Nebraska	2.42
4	Massachusetts	5.34	28	Arizona	2.36
5	Illinois	5.20	29	Montana	2.33
6	Connecticut	5.07	30	Idaho	2.23
7	New Jersey	4.70	31	Texas	2.10
8	Florida	4.26	32	Iowa	2.04
9	Maryland	4.25	33	Louisiana	2.03
10	Pennsylvania	4.14	34	West Virginia	1.95
11	Michigan	4.02	35	South Dakota	1.80
12	Washington	3.89	36	Kansas	1.80
13	Delaware	3.88	37	New Mexico	1.68
14	Rhode Island	3.80	38	Oklahoma	1.60
15	Wyoming	3.78	39	North Dakota	1.54
16	Oregon	3.53	40	Virginia	1.50
17	Ohio	3.50	41	Tennessee	1.44
18	Wisconsin	3.44	42	Kentucky	1.30
19	New Hampshire	3.36	43	North Carolina	1.24
20	Colorado	3.32	44	Georgia	1.17
21	Missouri	2.84	45	Alabama	1.13
22	Utah	2.64	46	Arkansas	1.02
23	Maine	2.49	47	Mississippi	.96
24	Indiana	2.47	48	South Carolina	.76
	Average Ten Southern States	1.43		Average Rest of Country	4.01

TABLE II

Comparison of Annual Current Income Per Capita, Ten Southern States and Remainder of Country.*

Calendar Years 1919-1921

Year	Annual Current Income Per Capita		Percentage South to Rest of Country
	Southern States	Rest of Country	
1919	$378	$691	54.7
1920	348	760	45.8
1921	369	877	42.0

*Source: Leven, *Income in the Various States*, National Bureau of Economic Research, New York, 1925, pp. 249 and 253.

mation is supplied as to the manner in which individual incomes are distributed around the general average, nor are any means afforded for measuring income differentials applicable to specific industries and occupations.

In order to understand why the general level of income in the South is low, it is necessary to know something about the particular forms of gainful activity which constitute the South's chief means of support, and to compare the returns received from such activities with the returns yielded by similar activities in other parts of the country. For this purpose recourse must be had to the data compiled by the Bureau of the Census and other governmental agencies covering the operations of specific industries.

CHAPTER II

PRODUCTIVITY AND WAGES IN SOUTHERN AGRICULTURE

IT HAS already been pointed out that the South is overwhelmingly agricultural. In four of the states under consideration, North Carolina, South Carolina, Mississippi, and Arkansas, over half of the total population lived on farms in 1925. Of the total number of persons gainfully employed in the southern area as a whole, 52.6 per cent were engaged in agriculture in 1920. The corresponding ratio for the rest of the country was only 20.4 per cent. Since agriculture constitutes the main source of livelihood of such a large proportion of the southern population, it is obvious that per capita agricultural productivity has an important bearing not only upon the incomes received by the farming classes, but, indirectly, upon the incomes of other classes of the population as well.

TABLE III

Comparison of Annual Gross Agricultural Income Per Worker, Ten Southern States and Remainder of Country.*

Year	Basis of All Workers Employed			Basis of Adult Male Workers		
	Ten Southern States	Remainder of United States	Percentage South is of Rest of Country	Ten Southern States	Remainder of United States	Percentage South is of Rest of Country
1899..	$189	$471	40.1	$334	$595	56.2
1909..	318	925	34.3	648	1,214	53.4
1919..	1,059	2,569	41.2	1,656	2,993	55.3
1924..	591	1,582	37.4	925	1,844	50.1
1927..	609	1,611	37.8	953	1,879	50.7

*For the derivation of the results shown in this table, see the section on methodology at the end of this chapter.

GROSS FARM INCOME PER WORKER

That agriculture yields a much lower return per farm worker in the South than it does in the rest of the country is decisively demonstrated by the data exhibited in Table III. This table has been compiled partly on the basis of census data and partly from information supplied by the Department of Agriculture. A detailed explanation of the methods used in arriving at the final results is given at the close of this chapter. No high degree of accuracy can be claimed for the amounts which purport to show the gross value of farm products per worker. For the purpose in view, however, it is the ratios between the South and the rest of the country which are important, and it is believed that these ratios reflect the comparative situation with a fair measure of precision, since most of the errors and omissions which affect the absolute totals are probably present to the same extent in both of the areas under comparison.

It will be seen from Table III that the gross value of farm products per adult male worker gainfully employed in southern agriculture has averaged but little above one-half of the corresponding value for the rest of the country during the last 28 years. In view of the importance of agriculture in southern economy, this fact goes far to explain why the general level of income in the South is low.

WAGES OF FARM LABORERS

If southern agriculture yields a gross return per worker only half as great as the average for the rest of the country, this circumstance should be expected to exercise an important influence upon the rate of wages paid hired farm labor. According to the Census of Occupations, there were in the southern area as a whole, in 1920, some 430,000 male persons, 18 years of age or over, belonging to the class of farm laborers working out. That these farm laborers formed no insignificant portion of the southern working population is indicated by the fact that their total number amounted to more than half of the number of male workers of all ages employed in manufacturing establishments in the same area in 1919. The farm laborers in question were by no means all Negroes. According to the census, about 45 per cent of them were whites. Although their number has undoubtedly fallen off considerably since 1920, farm laborers still constitute one of the major working class groups in the South.

How do the wages of farm laborers in the South compare with the average wages paid similar kinds of workers in other parts of the country? Does the farm wage differential correspond to the differential in per worker agricultural productivity? Answers to these questions are supplied by Table IV, which gives data on the average wages of hired farm hands in the various states of the union as collected by agents of the Department of Agriculture. It will be noted that as of July, 1929, the average cash wage of casual farm laborers ranged from $1.20 per day in South Carolina to $2.05 per day in Virginia. The median of the state averages for the ten southern states under consideration was $1.55 per day. The median of the state averages in the remainder of the United States was $3.25 per day. The wages of casual farm laborers in the South, in other words, amounted, on the average, to only 48 per cent of the wages paid elsewhere.

Hired farm laborers frequently receive certain perqui-

TABLE IV

Average Wages of Male Farm Laborers, by States.

State	Rank	Laborers, Not Boarded, Average Wages Per Day, July 1929*	Casual Farm Laborers, Average Cash Earnings Per Day Plus Perquisites, Year 1926**	Non-Casual Farm Laborers, Monthly Earnings Plus Perquisites, Year 1925**
Ten Southern States				
South Carolina	1	$1.20	$1.97	$46.84
Georgia	2	1.30	2.09	51.30
Alabama	3	1.40	2.26	50.65
Louisiana	4	1.50	2.33	52.89
Mississippi	5	1.55	2.59	63.58
Tennessee	6	1.55	2.19	51.69
Arkansas	7	1.65	2.41	56.60
Florida	8	1.65	2.66	69.55
North Carolina	9	1.80	2.54	57.19
Virginia	10	2.05	2.99	61.79
Median, South		$1.55	$2.37	$53.82
Remaining States				
Kentucky	1	$1.80	$2.90	$60.56
Texas	2	1.95	3.26	71.43
Oklahoma	3	2.05	4.16	65.68
Missouri	4	2.20	3.48	66.40
New Mexico	5	2.20	3.42	64.57
West Virginia	6	2.30	3.25	72.44
Arizona	7	2.75	3.00	72.50
Delaware	8	2.75	3.88	76.76
Indiana	9	2.75	4.38	75.24
Maryland	10	2.75	4.04	70.47
Illinois	11	2.90	5.10	83.22
Colorado	12	3.05	5.21	81.99
Ohio	13	3.05	4.45	73.58
Maine	14	3.10	4.98	80.13
Iowa	15	3.15	5.42	82.89
Minnesota	16	3.20	4.73	77.20
Oregon	17	3.20	3.95	95.93
Nevada	18	3.25	4.58	138.62
North Dakota	19	3.25	5.58	82.25
Pennsylvania	20	3.25	4.16	80.73
Wisconsin	21	3.25	4.08	78.98
Utah	22	3.25	4.09	93.90
South Dakota	23	3.30	5.23	80.81
Kansas	24	3.35	5.21	77.60
Michigan	25	3.35	4.04	79.89
Nebraska	26	3.35	5.19	77.12
Vermont	27	3.35	4.12	83.59
Wyoming	28	3.45	4.24	92.91
Idaho	29	3.50	4.67	100.51
California	30	3.55	4.56	115.51
New Jersey	31	3.55	5.22	95.89
New Hampshire	32	3.60	4.15	92.30
Washington	33	3.65	4.85	95.26
Montana	34	3.70	4.97	93.30
Massachusetts	35	3.80	4.12	93.30
Connecticut	36	3.85	4.20	89.03
New York	37	3.85	4.96	88.45
Rhode Island	38	3.85	3.93	95.07
Median		$3.25	$4.31	$81.40
Percentage South is of Rest of Country		47.7	54.9	66.1

**Monthly Labor Review*, Sept. 1929, p. 173.
***Yearbook of Agriculture*, 1928, pp. 1059 and 1060.

sites in addition to their money wages. The Department of Agriculture has compiled estimates of the average cash value of such perquisites in each of the several states for the years 1925 and 1926. If the value of perquisites be added to the cash earnings, the disparity between farm wages in the South and the rest of the country is somewhat lessened but it is nevertheless considerable. Thus it will be seen from Table IV that the average wage, including perquisites, of casual farm laborers in the median southern state in 1926 was $2.37 per day, which represented about 55 per cent of the corresponding average for the rest of the country.

Non-casual farm laborers probably represent the most skilled and experienced workers of their class. It will be seen from Table IV that the average monthly compensation, including perquisites, of this type of laborer in the median southern state was $54 in 1925, which represented 66 per cent of the corresponding average for the rest of the country. Summarizing the evidence furnished by Table IV, it may be said that the differential in farm wages as between the South and the rest of the country is in substantial accord with the differential in agricultural productivity, although the relationship seems to weaken in the case of the more experienced workers.

METHODOLOGY

No recent statistics are available bearing upon the amount of net income derived from agriculture in the various states. The Census of Agriculture, however, furnishes estimates, by divisions and states, of the gross value of farm products. These gross production figures are admittedly incomplete. Moreover, they contain certain elements of duplication, the most serious of which is the double counting of crops fed to livestock. An attempt was made to eliminate this duplication in the Census of 1900, but the effort was abandoned in subsequent reports.

Comprehensive information on the value of farm products cannot be obtained from the Census of Agriculture beyond the year 1919. The Census of 1925, for instance, gives merely the values of crops and livestock products, omitting the value of animals sold or slaughtered. Information compiled annually by the Department of Agriculture may, however, be utilized from the point where the census material leaves off. Thus the Department of Agriculture publishes annual estimates of the gross income derived from farming operations after making deductions for products fed to livestock, used for seed, or wasted. These estimates apply to the nation as a whole, but certain supplementary data are available which permit the national totals to be allocated between the South and the rest of the country.

Table A sets forth the estimated gross value of all farm products in the ten southern states under consideration and in the remainder of the country for the years 1899, 1909, 1919, 1924, and 1927. The figures for 1899, 1909, and 1919 have been obtained from the Census of Agriculture. As has already been indicated, the 1899 totals represent values reached after deducting the estimated value of crops fed to livestock. This is not true of the census estimates for 1909 and 1919. The figures for 1924 and 1927 represent an allocation between the South and the rest of the country of the Department of Agriculture's national totals for gross farm income.[1] The method used in making this allocation is shown in Table B.

[1] See *Yearbook of Agriculture,* 1928, p. 1051, Table 525.

TABLE A

Gross Value of Farm Products.

Year	Ten Southern States	Remainder of Country
1899	$ 715,600,000	$ 3,048,578,000
1909	1,565,335,000	6,928,895,000
1919	4,214,098,000	17,211,526,000
1924	2,076,040,000	9,926,960,000
1927	2,138,980,000	10,114,020,000

As will be seen from Table B, the national total for gross farm income was split into three sub-totals, representing respectively income from crops, income from meat animals, and income from poultry and dairy products. The share of the South in each of these sub-totals was then separately computed. The basis of allocation in the case of income from crops was supplied by the Department of Agriculture's annual estimates, by states, of the gross value of all crops produced.[2] Before the estimates in question could be used, however, it was necessary to eliminate, as far as possible, the value of crops fed to livestock. The principal crops fed to animals are corn, oats, barley, and hay. The 1920 Census of Agriculture gives, by states, the average percentages of these crops which were neither sold nor held for sale by farmers in 1919. It was assumed that the unsold percentages represented crops fed to livestock, and that the percentages in question had not changed greatly since 1919. On the basis of these two assumptions, the percentages of the corn, oat, barley, and hay crops not sold in 1919 were applied to the values of the corresponding crops in 1924 and 1927. The values thus obtained were then subtracted from the Department of Agriculture's state estimates of

[2] See *Yearbook of Agriculture,* 1925, p. 1204; *ibid.,* 1928, p. 1037.

total crop production. After this deduction had been made, the ratio, which the value of crops produced in the ten southern states bore to the value of crops produced in the country at large, was computed and used to determine the share of the South in the total national income from crops.

TABLE B

Allocation of Gross Agricultural Income Between the South and the Rest of the Country.

Item	Gross Income for Entire Country as Estimated by Department of Agriculture in Millions		Percentage Allocated to Ten Southern States		Gross Income Allocated to Southern States in Thousands	
	1924	1927	1924	1927	1924	1927
Grains	$1,842	$1,636				
Fruits and Vegetables	1,333	1,453				
Cotton and Cotton Seed	1,719	1,458				
All Other	1,232	1,236				
Total Crops	$6,126	$5,783	24.33	26.70	$1,490,460	$1,544,060
Meat Animals	2,619	2,842	9.21	7.44	241,210	211,440
Dairy and Poultry Products	3,258	3,628	10.57	10.57	344,370	383,480
Total Income	12,003	12,253			$2,076,040	$2,138,980

In determining the share of the South in the country's total income from meat animals, the only available basis of allocation was the value of animals on farms, as estimated annually by the Department of Agriculture. This basis cannot be expected to give highly accurate results. Nevertheless, where large sections of the country are under consideration, there is an obvious correlation between the value of meat animals produced in a given area and the value of such animals on farms at a given date. The method used in

TABLE C

Percentage of Gross Income from Meat Animals Allocatable to the South.

	Farm Value, Jan. 1, 1927 (In thousands)		Weight**	Weighted Value		Percentage South is of Total
	Ten Southern States	Entire United States		Ten Southern States	Entire United States	
All Cattle	$163,716	$2,289,761				
Less Dairy Cattle	104,613	1,298,904				
Remainder	$ 59,103	$990,857				
Plus ¼ Dairy Cattle*	26,153	324,726				
Total	$85,256	$1,315,583	.70	$59,679	$920,908	
Hogs	83,092	945,093	1.60	134,243	1,512,149	
Sheep	6,821	432,619	.50	3,410	216,310	
Grand Total				$197,332	$2,649,367	7.44

*Estimates of the Department of Agriculture indicate that approximately one-fourth of the total beef and veal supply of the country is furnished by dairy cattle and dairy calves. The value of dairy cattle has, therefore, been given a weight of one-quarter as against the value of beef cattle.

**Statistics published by the Department of Agriculture indicate that the value of beef and veal animals produced in 1924 represented 70 per cent of the weighted value of beef and veal animals on farms as of January 1, of that year. The value of hogs produced in 1924 represented 160 per cent of the value of hogs on farms as of January 1, and, finally, the value of sheep produced represented approximately 50 per cent of the value of sheep on farms as of the first of the year. See *Yearbook of Agriculture*, 1924, p. 961, Table 573.

determining the percentage of the total income from meat animals allocatable to the South in 1927 is illustrated in Table C.

As has already been indicated, the Census of Agriculture for 1925 gives the value of livestock products by states for the year 1924. On the basis of this data it was possible to obtain directly the percentage of the total income from poultry and dairy products allocatable to the South in 1924. The same percentage was used for 1927, on the assumption that there had been no change during the intervening two years.

In order to compare the per capita agricultural productivity of the South with that of the rest of the country, it was necessary to divide the gross values produced in each section by the number of persons employed in agricultural pursuits. The total numbers of persons gainfully employed in agriculture for the years 1900, 1910, and 1920 were obtained from the Census of Occupations. Approximate estimates of the numbers employed in 1924 and 1927 were calculated on the basis of the percentage decline in farm population between 1920 and 1925 as reported by the Census of Agriculture.

The Census of Occupations reports as gainfully employed in agriculture many women and children whose contribution to the total agricultural product may be exceedingly slight. The South, due to its large Negro population, employs a considerably greater proportion of women and children on farms than does the rest of the country. To compute the average product per worker on the basis of figures which include persons of both sexes and of all ages will consequently unduly depress the southern average. The work of women and children, as a general rule, merely supplements the work of adult males, and for this reason it is possibly preferable to limit consideration to the latter class of workers. To disregard the labor of women and children entirely will, however, result in somewhat exaggerating the southern average. The proper method would, of course, be to equate the women and children to their equivalent in terms of adult males. Since there is no way of doing this, both bases of calculation were used in the present study. Table D gives the data on the number of agricultural workers employed upon which these calculations were based.

TABLE D

Number of Persons Gainfully Employed in Agriculture, Ten Southern States and Remainder of Country.

Year	Both Sexes and All Ages		Adult Males**	
	Ten Southern States	Remainder of Country	Ten Southern States	Remainder of Country
1900	3,794,486	6,479,183	2,142,116	5,125,884
1910	4,927,906	7,489,491	2,416,380	5,708,745
1920	3,978,306	6,704,638	2,544,231	5,750,933
1924*	3,510,457	6,276,212	2,245,029	5,383,448
1927*	3,510,457	6,276,212	2,245,029	5,383,448

*Estimated by applying the percentage decline in farm population between 1920 and 1925, to the 1920 totals for agricultural workers.

**Figures for 1900 and 1910 represent all male workers twenty-one years of age or over. Figures for later years represent male workers 20 years or over.

CHAPTER III

THE WAGE DIFFERENTIAL IN SOUTHERN INDUSTRY

PROBLEMS connected with the growth of southern industry have received so much attention in recent years that it is easy to lose sight of the fact that the South is still one of the most agricultural regions in the United States. In 1920, for every Southerner engaged in manufacturing and mechanical pursuits, there were three Southerners engaged in farming. In the rest of the country the situation was almost reversed. For every person engaged in agriculture there were 1.6 persons in the manufacturing and mechanical employments. The emphasis placed on southern industry is, nevertheless, amply justified by the extraordinary rapidity with which it is expanding. Outside of the South, the number of wage earners employed in manufacturing establishments declined by some 9 per cent between 1919 and 1927. In the ten southern states under consideration the number of factory employees increased by 9 per cent during the same period. Further light on the drift toward industry in the South is furnished by the relative rate of decline of the farm population. Between 1920 and 1925 the southern farm population experienced a reduction of 11.8 per cent, as compared with a reduction of only 6.4 per cent for the rest of the country.[1]

Roughly speaking, about one and one-half million per-

[1] The figures on farm population for 1925 are not strictly comparable with those reported in 1920, since the definition used in 1920 included not only persons living on farms but, in addition, those farm laborers and their families who, while not living on farms, did live in rural territory outside any incorporated places.

sons are gainfully employed in manufacturing and mechanical industries in the South. This constitutes about 18 per cent of the total working population. Except for agriculture, which is rapidly losing ground, industry supports a larger percentage of the southern population than any other gainful activity. The relative adequacy of this support as compared with standards attained in other sections of the country is, therefore, of considerable moment.

Of the total number of Southerners engaged in manufacturing and mechanical pursuits, somewhat over a million are factory wage earners. A rough measure of the relative level of income obtaining among these employees is supplied by the Census of Manufactures, which gives, by states, the average number of wage earners employed during the year as well as the total amount expended for wages. Division of the amount spent for wages by the number of workers employed gives an annual average wage which, within limits to be noted further on, may be taken as a fairly accurate index of the variation in average industrial earnings as between different sections of the country.

THE CENSUS AVERAGE WAGE

Table V gives a comparison of the average census wage in the ten southern states under consideration with the corresponding average for the rest of the country. This table seems to indicate that the average earnings of southern factory workers have been from 30 to 40 per cent lower than the earnings of similar classes of employees in other parts of the country for a long period of years. Before attaching too much significance to this evidence, however, it is in order to inquire into its limitations.

TABLE V

Comparison of Census Average Wage, Ten Southern States and Remainder of Country.

Year	Census Average Wage		Percentage South is of Rest of Country
	Ten Southern States	Remainder of United States	
1849..........	$197	$252	77.9
1859..........	257	292	87.9
1869..........	215	389	55.4
1899..........	272	445	61.3
1904..........	337	495	68.1
1914..........	410	601	68.2
1919..........	884	1,196	73.9
1921..........	792	1,229	64.4
1923..........	794	1,313	60.5
1925..........	832	1,339	62.1
1927..........	828	1,366	60.6

The objection may legitimately be raised that the census average wages, as calculated in Table V, reflect neither average annual earnings nor rates of pay for comparable kinds of work. In the first place the wages in question are simply arithmetic results obtained by dividing the aggregate annual amount spent for wages by the average number of workers employed. The average number of workers employed is obtained by dividing by 12 the sum of the numbers reported on the payrolls as of the 15th day of each month. It is plain that the census average wage does not measure the actual average earnings of the workers attached to a given industry. It merely indicates what would have been their average per capita earnings if production schedules had been so arranged as to give them continuous employment throughout the year. The possible error involved in using the census average wage as a measure of per capita earnings may be illustrated by a simple example.

Let it be supposed that two industries have identical wage bills of $1,000,000 per annum. The first industry operates with a stable working force of 1,000 employees throughout the year. The second industry operates with 1,200 employees for six months of the year and with a force of 800 employees during the remaining months. According to the method of calculation used by the Census of Manufactures, both industries will have an average working force of 1,000 employees. Both industries will, therefore, have the same census average wage of $1,000. However, unless the workers, laid off in the second industry, find equally remunerative employment elsewhere, the average actual earnings of the workers attached to that industry will be considerably below the average of the industry which provides stable all year round employment.

IS THE CENSUS WAGE SIGNIFICANT?

It is evident that variations in the census wage averages as between different industries reflect corresponding variations in average actual earnings only when there is substantial similarity with respect to the ratio which the total number of workers attached to each industry bears to the average number of workers it employs during the year. Translated into concrete terms, this requirement means that the average amount of unemployment per worker, in each of the industries under consideration, must be the same. In an industry which has no reserve of unemployed labor, and which gives continuous work to all of its employees throughout the year, the census average wage constitutes an accurate measure of average actual earnings. On the other hand, in an industry which habitually has a large reserve of unemployed labor, and in which few workers have continuous employment throughout the year, the census average wage may be considerably higher than the actual earnings per worker.

The question therefore arises, as to whether the industries of the South are sufficiently like those of the rest of the country, with respect to the factor of employment stability, to justify using the percentages shown in Table V as measures of the relative difference in actual per capita earnings. That no material error is involved in assuming such similarity is indicated by the results of a study made by Professor Paul F. Brissenden for the United States Bureau of the Census. Professor Brissenden supplies carefully worked out estimates, by states, of the average actual earnings of industrial wage earners for the census years 1899 to 1923.[2] When the census wage averages shown in Table V are replaced by the estimated actual earnings, as computed from Professor Brissenden's data, little change in the percentage relation between the South and the rest of the country is found to result. For instance, when such substitutions are made for the year 1923, the ratio between the South and the rest of the country changes no more than from 60.5 per cent to 61.7 per cent. The same procedure followed out with respect to the year 1919 changes the ratio given in Table V from 73.9 to 70.8 per cent.

A second objection, which may be raised against the accuracy of the comparison given in Table V, is that no allowance has been made for a possible difference in the proportion of women and children in the two wage earning groups under consideration. Since women and children

[2] "Earnings of Factory Workers, 1899 to 1927," *Census Monographs*, *X*, p. 107, Table 42.

normally receive lower wages than adult males, it is evident that the group having the higher percentage of women and children will have a lower average of per capita earnings, even though the two groups are on a basis of parity with respect to the earnings of their adult males. In order to secure a valid comparison, it is necessary to reduce each group to the same footing as regards age and sex distribution. That a correction of this kind would have little effect on the percentages shown in Table V is indicated by data which are available with respect to the census year, 1919.

In that year, approximately 15.2 per cent of the wage earners in southern establishments were women over 16 years of age, and 1.8 per cent were children of both sexes under sixteen years. The comparable percentages for the remainder of the country were 20.2 per cent and 1.3 per cent respectively. Professor Brissenden estimates that the average full-time earnings of women factory workers in 1919 were about 54 per cent as great as the earnings of adult males, and that the per capita earnings of children under sixteen years of age averaged around 30 per cent of the earnings of adult males.[8] This information makes it possible to recalculate the census wage averages for 1919 on the basis of wage earning groups composed exclusively of adult males. As thus revised, the census average wage for the South is found to represent 72.3 per cent of the comparable average for the rest of the country, instead of 73.9 per cent as shown in Table V. This difference is too small to have any importance from the standpoint of the present study.

It may be objected, finally, that Table V attempts to compare the earnings of workers engaged in widely dis-

[8] *Census Monographs, X*, p. 297, Table 134.

similar industries and occupations. This is perfectly true. The table in question simply shows how average earnings in the particular types of employment open to southern wage earners compare with earnings in the particular occupations open to wage earners outside of the South. It cannot and does not purport to measure the relative differences in rates of pay for comparable kinds of work.

It is apparent that none of the limitations of Table V are sufficiently potent to discredit its main testimony, which is that the average annual earnings of industrial workers in the South are, roughly speaking, about 40 per cent below the average obtaining in other parts of the country. This information is important as far as it goes, but it does not go far enough. To what extent is the lower average of southern earnings due to a lower scale of wages for comparable kinds of work? To what extent is it due to other factors such as, for instance, a preponderance of industries which normally employ large numbers of unskilled workers? Data bearing on the first of these questions are given in the remaining sections of the present chapter. The second question is touched upon in Chapter V.

SPECIFIC INDUSTRIES

The bulk of the industrial wage earners of the South are concentrated in a comparatively small number of industries. By all odds the most important activity, from the standpoint of the number of workers employed, is the manufacture of textiles. Southern cotton goods establishments employed about 271,000 wage workers in 1927. Knit goods establishments employed about 50,000 workers. All told, nearly a third of the total number of southern industrial wage earners were attached to the textile industry in 1927.

Next in importance to textiles as a source of employment is the lumber and timber industry. About 215,000 wage earners, or slightly more than one-fifth of the total number of southern industrial workers, were engaged in this industry in 1927. None of the remaining industries of the South stand out with any particular degree of prominence as regards number of workers employed. A possible exception are steam railroad repair shops, the operation of which required the services of approximately 60,000 persons in 1927. This was the only southern industry, aside from textiles and timber products, which gave employment to more than 40,000 persons in 1927.

The wage comparisons which follow are confined in the main to the few important industries enumerated above. This limitation was necessary because of the lack of adequate data on other industries. The wage statistics presented, however, cover nearly 60 per cent of all workers engaged in manufacturing activities in the South.

Table VI gives a comparison between the South and the rest of the country of the census wage averages obtaining

TABLE VI

Comparison of Census Wage Averages in Specified Industries, Ten Southern States and Elsewhere. Census Year 1927.*

	Census Average Wage		Percentage Southern Average is of Average Elsewhere
	South	Elsewhere	
Knit Goods	$655	$1,099	59.6
Cotton Goods	671	1,012	66.3
Lumber and Timber	748	1,195	62.5
Foundry and Machine Shops	1,230	1,495	80.4
Railroad Repair Shops	1,376	1,537	89.5

*Source: *Census of Manufactures, 1927.*

respectively in the cotton goods industry, the lumber and timber industry, the knit goods industry, foundry and machine shops, and railroad repair shops. It appears from this table that the wage differential between the South and the rest of the country is markedly reduced when consideration is limited to comparable industries. As indicated in Table V, the general census wage average for the South in 1927 represented only 60.6 per cent of the corresponding general average for the rest of the country. The wage ratios applicable to the specific industries shown in Table VI are in all but one instance greater than this figure, ranging from 59.6 per cent in the knit goods industry to 89.5 per cent in the case of railroad repair shops. That there should be a greater disparity in the general average of industrial wages, as between the South and elsewhere, than in the wage averages applicable to specific industries may at first sight seem curious. As is more fully explained in Chapter V, however, this apparent anomaly is due to the fact that the dominant industries of the South are low-wage industries, whereas, outside of the South, there are many high-wage industries which are either very weakly represented in the South or not represented there at all.

The fact that the percentage ratios between the southern wage averages and the corresponding averages for the rest of the country are subject to considerable variation from industry to industry is another circumstance which calls for explanation. Why should the wages of southern workers in the knit goods industry, for instance, have averaged less than 60 per cent of the average obtaining among the same class of workers elsewhere, while wages in southern railroad repair shops averaged nearly 90 per cent of the corresponding average elsewhere?

The variations in question are probably due in part to the fact that the industrial classifications used are extremely broad and include establishments which differ considerably with respect to the type of their product and the character of their manufacturing operations. Within the same industry, there may be found, at one extreme, establishments which specialize on products requiring the employment of a high proportion of skilled workers; and, at the other extreme, establishments the manufacturing operations of which are such as to require a relatively small proportion of skilled workers. In the first class of establishments, the average census wage will naturally be high. The second class of establishments will have a relatively low census wage average. In an industry, the southern branch of which has more than its proportionate share of the latter class of establishments, a disparity in the census wage averages as between the South and the rest of the country is bound to appear, even though there are no differences in rates of pay for comparable kinds of work. The relative distribution of the high and low wage establishments, as between the South and elsewhere, will not, of course, be the same for all industries. This circumstance probably accounts in part for the differences in the wage spreads shown in Table VI.

There is very little information at hand on which to base an estimate of the extent to which the lower census wage averages of southern industries are due to a larger representation of establishments, the manufacturing processes of which require a relatively small proportion of skilled workers. There is direct evidence, however, that this factor is responsible for the extremely broad wage spread between the southern and northern divisions of the knit goods industry.

The most important product of this industry is hosiery, of which there are two main types, seamless and full-fashioned. Full-fashioned hosiery workers represent on the whole a more highly remunerated group of employees than workers on seamless hosiery. Thus, a shift by Massachusetts hosiery mills, from the manufacture of seamless to the manufacture of full-fashioned hosiery, was in large part responsible for an increase in the average earnings of male hosiery workers in that state from 47 cents per hour in 1926 to $1.15 per hour in 1928.[4] The number of full-fashioned hosiery mills in the South is relatively small, and this circumstance undoubtedly serves to exaggerate the difference in average wages as between the southern and northern branches of the knit goods industry.

Another circumstance, which partially explains the variations, as between industries, in the wage ratios shown in Table VI, is the fact that the industries under comparison differ with respect to the factor of geographical location. For instance, outside of the South, the lumber and timber industry is concentrated mainly in the Pacific Coast States. These states have on the whole a very high regional level of wages. Even within the southern area, there are considerable variations from state to state in the general level of wages. In the cotton textile industry, for instance, average hourly earnings, for a representative pay period in 1928,

[4] *Bulletin of the United States Bureau of Labor Statistics, No. 504,* p. 10.

were 31.6 cents in Virginia, 29.5 cents in North Carolina, 26.0 cents in South Carolina and Georgia, and 24.4 cents in Alabama.[5] When an industry is located in an area of high wages in the North and in an area of low wages in the South, the wage differential between its two divisions will naturally be greater than if the situation were reversed. The factor of geographical location, as a cause of industrial variations in the disparity between southern and northern wage averages, is of comparatively slight importance, however, in comparison with another factor which is brought to light when the wage differentials applicable to specific occupations within the several industries are compared.

SPECIFIC OCCUPATIONS AND EMPLOYMENTS

The United States Bureau of Labor Statistics has collected sample data by states relative to the hourly earnings of workers engaged in specific occupations and employments in a number of important industries. These industries include cotton goods, hosiery and underwear (knit goods), lumber and timber, and foundry and machine shop products. The census wage averages for all of the above industries have been given in Table VI. Tables VII, VIII, IX, and X, which are based on the data compiled by the Bureau of Labor Statistics, give average hourly earnings in the more important occupations included within these industries. They also show, by occupations, the relative level of southern earnings of pay as compared with the level of earnings elsewhere.

A cursory examination of these tables indicates that there is no uniform relation between the average wages paid in

[5] *Bulletin of the United States Bureua of Labor Statistics, No. 492,* p. 8.

various occupations in the South and the wages prevailing in similar occupations in other parts of the country. The wage ratio between the South and elsewhere ranges, in fact, all the way from 51 per cent, in the case of sorters in sawmills, to 104 per cent, in the case of certain classes of machinists. A further tendency to be noted is the apparent relationship between the size of the wage differential and the factor of skill. As will be seen, the difference in hourly earnings between the South and the rest of the country is apparently at a maximum in the case of common labor and shows a tendency to become progressively less with each advance in the grade of skill. In the case of one or two highly skilled occupations it disappears entirely. This tendency is not particularly pronounced as regards industries in which differences in grades of skill are slight and in which advancement from one occupation to another is comparatively easy. It is strikingly evident, however, in industries in which there are broad differences in skill as between various occupational groups and in which passage from one group to another is difficult.

In the cotton goods and hosiery and underwear industries, which are covered in Tables VII and VIII respectively, the correlation between the degree of occupational skill and the size of the wage differential is not as clearly apparent as in the case of the lumber and timber industry or of foundry and machine shops. This circumstance is attributable to a variety of factors. In the first place, the gradations of skill which separate the various occupations of the textile industry are for the most part very slight. A majority of the occupations may be mastered in a relatively short period of time. Employees in certain occupations are remunerated on a piece-rate basis. In other occupations a time-rate basis is used. Generally speaking, the differential in hourly earnings, as between the South and elsewhere, is somewhat smaller in the piece-rate than it is in the time-rate occupations. Another factor, which has to be reckoned with, is the circumstance that certain textile occupations are carried on primarily by males in the South, whereas in the North they are carried on primarily by females.

Despite disturbing influences such as these, the tendency of the wage differential to vary with the degree of skill is observable to a certain extent even in the textile industry. Reference to the figures for male workers in the cotton goods industry given in Table VII, for instance, shows that the only occupations markedly out of line with the tendency noted are those of doffers and weavers. It is significant that the remuneration in both of these occupations is normally based on piece rates whereas the other occupations are generally on a time-rate basis.

The relationship between the size of the wage differential and the skill of the occupation, as measured by the rate of compensation received, is displayed more prominently in the sawmill industry, data on which are given in Table IX. It will be noted that the average level of southern wages in occupations which yield less than 30 cents an hour, ranges from 51 per cent to 62 per cent of the corresponding wage level elsewhere. Southern wages in occupations which yield from 30 to 40 cents per hour range from 62 per cent to 70 per cent of the prevailing wages elsewhere. Graders in the South receive an average of 42 cents per hour, which is 76.5 per cent as great as the average earnings of graders in the rest of the

TABLE VII

Comparison of Average Hourly Earnings in Cotton Goods Manufacturing, Five Southern and Six Northern States, October 1928.*

Occupational Classification	Southern States		Northern States		Percentage Southern Earnings are of Northern
	Number of Empls. Covered	Average Hourly Earnings	Number of Empls. Covered	Average Hourly Earnings	
Males:					
Picker Tenders	774	$.232	397	$.380	61.1
Card Tenders and Strippers	1,151	.260	606	.416	62.5
Doffers	3,013	.280	932	.411	68.1
Speeder Tenders	2,415	.317	498	.483	65.6
Slubber Tenders	768	.317	336	.475	66.7
Weavers	5,738	.341	4,588	.456	74.8
Loom Fixers	2,089	.399	1,452	.602	66.3
Females:					
Trimmers or Inspectors	1,113	.208	1,142	.273	76.2
Spooler Tenders	3,119	.209	1,498	.314	66.6
Spinners, Frame	6,962	.228	3,456	.373	61.1
Drawers-in, Hand	453	.283	537	.363	78.0
Speeder Tenders	722	.285	2,273	.383	74.4
Weavers	3,759	.308	4,364	.425	72.5

*Source: *Bulletin of the United States Bureau of Labor Statistics, No. 492*, p. 26. The five southern states comprise Alabama, Georgia, North Carolina South Carolina, and Virginia; the six northern states, Connecticut, Maine, Massachusetts, New Hampshire, New York, and Rhode Island. With the exception of female drawers-in, only occupations represented by 1000 or more employees have been included in the above table.

TABLE VIII

Comparison of Average Hourly Earnings in the Hosiery and Underwear Industry, 1928.*

Occupational Classification	Southern States		Northern States		Percentage Southern Earnings are of Northern
	Number of Empls. Covered	Average Hourly Earnings	Number of Empls. Covered	Average Hourly Earnings	
HOSIERY					
MALES:					
Boarders	776	$.381	657	$.686	55.5
Machine Fixers	444	.635	366	.912	69.6
FEMALES:					
Inspectors	809	.226	1,088	.378	59.8
Menders	380	.232	914	.452	51.3
Knitters, Transfer	1,355	.232	1,128	.368	63.1
Loopers	1,201	.245	2,406	.414	59.2
Pairers or Maters	436	.272	783	.420	64.7
Folders	261	.280	334	.381	73.5
Winders	238	.317	453	.392	80.9
UNDERWEAR					
MALES:					
Knitters, Web or Tube	89	.408	357	.510	80.0
Machine Fixers	33	.595	190	.751	79.2
FEMALES:					
Inspectors	248	.220	1,066	.292	75.3
Cutters, Hand, Layers-up and Markers	64	.251	391	.359	69.9
Buttonhole Makers	74	.262	295	.361	72.5
Folders	112	.266	376	.366	72.6
Seamers	415	.269	2,010	.373	72.1
Finishers	422	.270	2,753	.352	76.7

*Source: *Bulletin of the United States Bureau of Labor Statistics, No. 504*, p. 42. For the underwear industry, the states compared are North Carolina, Tennessee, and Virginia in the South, and Connecticut, Rhode Island, Illinois, Indiana, Massachusetts, Michigan, Minnesota, Wisconsin, New Hampshire, Vermont, New York, and Pennsylvania in the North. For the hosiery industry, the southern states comprise Alabama and Louisiana, Georgia, North Carolina, Tennessee, and Virginia; the northern, Illinois, Indiana, Maryland, West Virginia, Massachusetts, Michigan, Minnesota, Wisconsin, New Hampshire, Vermont, New Jersey, New York, and Pennsylvania. Only the more important occupations, in which employees could be segregated by states, have been included in the above table.

TABLE IX

Comparison of Average Hourly Earnings in Sawmills, Ten Southern and Twelve Other States, 1928.*

Occupational Classification	Southern States		Other States		Percentage Southern Earnings to Those Elsewhere
	Number of Empls. Covered	Average Hourly Earnings	Number of Empls. Covered	Average Hourly Earnings	
Laborers	11,857	$.219	10,169	$.401	54.6
Off-Bearers	412	.222	448	.404	55.0
Edger Tailers	315	.229	393	.391	58.6
Sorters	1,753	.230	2,385	.450	51.1
Transfer Men	337	.232	371	.440	52.7
Truckers	1,612	.240	1,525	.411	58.4
Saw Tailers	324	.256	414	.433	59.1
Pondmen	601	.259	743	.436	59.4
Doggers	544	.264	417	.427	61.8
Stackers, Hand	2,455	.270	1,862	.505	53.5
Machine Feeders, Planing	811	.272	971	.457	59.5
Tallymen	256	.326	424	.527	61.9
Edgermen	445	.367	476	.565	65.0
Setters	329	.376	413	.541	69.5
Graders	541	.419	1,021	.548	76.5
Millwrights	261	.524	440	.663	80.5
Sawyers, Head, Band	305	.831	363	.934	89.0

*Source: *Bulletin of the United States Bureau of Labor Statistics, No. 497*, p. 28. The ten southern states are Alabama, Arkansas, Florida, Georgia, Louisiana, Mississippi, North Carolina, South Carolina, Tennessee, and Virginia. The other states are California, Idaho, Kentucky, Maine, Michigan, Minnesota, Montana, Oregon, Texas, Washington, West Virginia, and Wisconsin. Only occupations represented by 650 or more employees have been included in the above table.

TABLE X

Comparison of Average Hourly Earnings in Foundries and Machine Shops, Four Southern and Twenty-four Other States, 1927.*

Occupational Classification	Southern States		Other States		Percentage Southern Earnings are of Earnings Elsewhere
	Number of Empls. Covered	Average Hourly Earnings	Number of Empls. Covered	Average Hourly Earnings	
FOUNDRIES:					
Laborers, Male	353	$.285	10,664	$.498	57.2
Chippers and Rough Grinders, Male	128	.311	3,729	.545	57.0
Molders' Helpers, Floor, Male	231	.325	1,589	.507	64.1
Core Makers, Male	105	.552	2,935	.762	72.4
Molders, Hand, Floor, Male	249	.708	5,126	.825	85.8
Pattern Makers, Male	48	.772	1,464	.832	92.8
MACHINE SHOPS:					
Laborers, Male	245	.289	8,097	.461	62.7
Blacksmiths' Helpers, Male	35	.383	687	.532	72.0
Machinists' Helpers, Male	60	.404	1,611	.514	78.6
Drill Press Hands, Male	69	.419	4,690	.608	68.9
Fitters and Bench Hands, Male	51	.439	6,610	.664	66.1
Assemblers, Male	61	.557	7,958	.654	85.2
Planer Hands, Male	22	.592	1,796	.744	79.6
Lathe Hands, Engine, Male	98	.615	5,866	.696	88.4
Boring-Mill Hands	35	.639	2,173	.728	87.8
Toolmakers, Male	23	.729	2,840	.756	96.4
Blacksmiths, Male	27	.744	818	.725	102.6
Machinists, Male	249	.754	3,545	.726	103,9
Pattern Makers, Male	21	.794	1,207	.842	94.3

*Source: *Bulletin of U. S. Bureau of Labor Statistics, No. 471*, p. 33. The southern states included in the comparison are Alabama, Georgia, Louisiana, and Tennessee. The remaining group comprises California, Colorado, Connecticut, Illinois, Indiana, Iowa, Kansas, Kentucky, Maine, Maryland, Massachusetts, Michigan, Minnesota, Missouri, New Hampshire, New Jersey, New York, Ohio, Oregon, Pennsylvania, Rhode Island, Texas, Washington, and Wisconsin.

country. Southern millwrights, with average earnings of 52 cents per hour, receive 80.5 per cent as much as the average earnings elsewhere. Finally, in the case of the highly skilled sawyers, whose average earnings in the South are 83 cents per hour, the ratio of southern wages to those paid elsewhere is 89 per cent.

Table X, which sets forth the comparative wage situation in foundries and machine shops, reveals similar tendencies. Thus, in foundries, the ratio of average southern earnings to average earnings elsewhere is 57 per cent in the case of common labor, 64 per cent in the case of semi-skilled molders' helpers, and 93 per cent in the case of the highly skilled pattern makers. In machine shops, the range of the same ratio extends from 63 per cent in the case of laborers to 104 per cent in the case of skilled machinists.

Since there is no uniform wage differential between the South and the rest of the country, and since the size of the wage differential with respect to any particular occupation depends largely on the factor of skill, it is easy to understand why average earnings for entire industries fall short of the corresponding averages for the rest of the country by varying degrees. In industries which employ a high proportion of unskilled workers, the disparity in average earnings between the South and elsewhere will naturally be high. In industries in which skilled workers predominate, the disparity in average earnings will be small. This fact goes far toward explaining why the average census wage for the southern lumber and timber industry is so low relative to the corresponding census average for the rest of the country, and why the census wage averages for railroad repair shops and foundry and machine shops are relatively high.

CHAPTER IV

MISCELLANEOUS WAGE AND SALARY DIFFERENTIALS

WAGE statistics covering employees in manufacturing establishments are by no means the only data which indicate that the differential between the South and the rest of the country reaches its maximum in unskilled employments and is at a minimum as regards occupations involving a high degree of skill. Table XI gives a comparison of the wages paid common laborers in eight different lines of activity, including casual labor on farms, common labor in sawmills, street cleaning and other unskilled work performed by laborers on city payrolls, labor on federal-aid road projects, common labor in foundries and in machine shops, and common labor in United States naval establishments. There are probably some differences as to the grade of labor utilized in the various activities mentioned. Moreover, the proportion of Negro workers is possibly greater in certain employments such as farming and sawmill operation than it is in others. The wage rates quoted in Table XI, however, apply in all cases to the lowest grade of adult male labor employed. In four of the employments listed, the basis of the wage comparison is hourly earnings. In the remaining four employments the basis used is hourly rates of pay. It is significant, therefore, that the table reveals an extremely broad spread, in every one of the employments enumerated, between the southern wage averages and those obtaining elsewhere. The difference is greatest in the case of casual farm labor, which in the South is largely performed by Negroes and which may there be obtained at less than half the average wage required in other parts of the country. In none of the activities specified, however, do the southern rates for common labor ever reach as high as 65 per cent of the rates prevailing elsewhere.

TABLE XI
Comparison of Average Wages for Common Labor, the South and Elsewhere.

Type of Employment	The South[1]	Elsewhere	Percentage Southern Wages are of Wages Elsewhere
Casual Farm Laborers, Not Boarded, Median of State Averages for Wages per Day, July, 1929[2]	$1.550	$3.250	47.7
Common Labor in Sawmills, Average Hourly Earnings, 1928[3]	.219	.401	54.6
Unskilled Street Laborers, Directly Hired by 369 Southern Cities and 2,257 Cities Elsewhere, Hourly Entrance Rate, Median City, 1928[4]	.255	.452	56.4
Common Laborers Employed on Federal Aid Road Projects, Average Hourly Rates, 1928[5]	.267	.445	60.7
Common Labor in Foundries, Average Hourly Earnings, 1927[6]	.285	.498	57.2
Common Labor in Machine Shops, Average Hourly Earnings, 1927[7]	.289	.461	62.7
Common Labor Employed in 13 Selected Industries, Average Hourly Entrance Rates, Jan. 1, 1929[8]	.291	.458	63.5
Common Labor in U. S. Naval Establishments, Three Southern and Seven Northern Ports, Hourly Rate at Median Port, 1929[9]	.360	.560	64.3

[1] Unless otherwise indicated the term "South" means Virginia, North Carolina, South Carolina, Georgia, Florida, Tennessee, Alabama, Mississippi, Arkansas, and Louisiana.
[2] For source see Table IV.
[3] For source see Table IX.
[4] Source: *Bulletin of the U. S. Bureau of Labor Statistics, No. 484*, p. 1.
[5] Source: *Yearbook of Agriculture*, 1928, p. 1105. For the purpose of this comparison the southern area includes, in addition to the ten states indicated above, the states of Delaware, Kentucky, Maryland, Oklahoma, Texas, and West Virginia.
[6] For source see Table X.
[7] For source see Table X.
[8] Source: *Monthly Labor Review*, May 1929, p. 189. This report gives average hourly entrance rates by geographic divisions. The rate for the South, as given in the above table, represents a weighted average of the averages for the South Atlantic and East South Central Divisions. The rate for the rest of the country represents a weighted average of the remaining divisional averages.
[9] For source see Table XIII.

TRADE UNION WAGE SCALES

Whereas common laborers rank near the bottom of the scale of skill, trade unionists may be placed near the top. The wages of trade unionists should, therefore, be expected to approach more closely the level prevailing in other parts of the country, and such statistics as are available do not disappoint this expectation. The United States Bureau of Labor Statistics makes an annual compilation of union wage scales obtaining in each of forty cities. Eight of these cities are located in what has been defined for the present purpose as the South. Table XII compares the rates of pay obtaining in the respective median cities of the South with the

TABLE XII

Comparison of Trade Union Wage Scales, Eight Southern Cities and Thirty-two Cities Located Outside of the South, May 15, 1929.*

Occupation	Hourly Rate of Pay, Median Southern City	Hourly Rate of Pay, Median City Elsewhere	Percentage Southern Rates are of Rates Elsewhere
Bricklayers	$1.500	$1.500	100.0
Carpenters	.900	1.200	75.0
Compositors, Book and Job	.920	1.023	89.9
Compositors, Day Work, Newspaper	1.000	1.145	87.3
Inside Wiremen	1.125	1.375	81.8
Painters	.875	1.125	77.8
Plasterers	1.250	1.500	83.3
Plumbers	1.250	1.375	90.9
Typesetting Machine Operators, Book and Job	.923	1.057	87.3
Typesetting Machine Operators, Newspaper	1.000	1.148	87.1
Unweighted Average	$1.074	$1.245	86.0

*Source: *Monthly Labor Review*, September, 1929, p. 144. The eight southern cities are Atlanta, Birmingham, Charleston, Jacksonville, Little Rock, Memphis, New Orleans, and Richmond. The thirty-two other cities comprise Baltimore, Boston, Buffalo, Chicago, Cincinnati Cleveland, Dallas, Denver, Detroit, Fall River, Indianapolis, Kansas City, Los Angeles, Louisville, Manchester, Milwaukee, Minneapolis, Newark, New Haven, New York, Omaha, Philadelphia, Pittsburg, Portland, Providence, St. Louis, St. Paul, Salt Lake City, San Francisco, Scranton, Seattle, and Washington.

corresponding averages applicable to the group of cities located outside of the South. It will be noted that in none of the trades listed is the representative southern rate more than 25 per cent below the corresponding figure for cities outside of the South. On the average, southern trade union wage rates are only 14 per cent below the level prevailing elsewhere, as contrasted with a differential ranging from 40 to 50 per cent in the case of common labor.

WAGES IN FEDERAL NAVAL ESTABLISHMENTS

That the tendencies discussed above are sufficiently strong to affect the wage policy of even so disinterested an employer as the United States government is indicated by Table XIII. The Federal government has ten naval establishments, three of which are located in the South. The operation of these establishments normally requires a considerable force of civil employees representing a wide variety of occupations and trades. Employees are divided into three groups or services on the basis of their skill and experience. The laborer service comprises unskilled common laborers. The helper service comprises semi-skilled assistants to skilled mechanics. The mechanical service comprises the class of skilled craftsmen. It will be noted from Table XIII that the ratio of the representative southern to the representative northern rate of pay is 64 per cent in the case of common laborers, 82 per cent in the case of mechanics' helpers, and 94 per cent in the case of skilled craftsmen. A comparison of the above percentages with those given in the preceding tables for employees of the same grades of skill would seem to indicate that the wage differentials between the South and the rest of the country are given substantially the same recognition by the United States Navy as they are by private employers.

TABLE XIII

Comparison of Hourly Wage Rates of Civil Employees in United States Naval Establishments, Three Southern and Seven Northern Ports. Year 1929.*

Occupation	Hourly Rate Median Southern Port	Hourly Rate Median Northern Port	Percentage Southern Rates are of Northern
GROUP I—Laborer Service:			
Laborer, Common	$ .36	$ .56	64.3
GROUP II—Helper Service:			
Electrician	.51	.63	81.0
Machinist	.51	.61	83.6
Pipe Fitter	.51	.63	81.0
Rigger	.51	.61	83.6
Unweighted Average	$ .51	$ .62	82.3
GROUP III—Mechanical Service:			
Boiler Maker	$ .82	$ .88	93.2
Calker and Chipper, Iron	.82	.89	92.1
Cement Finisher	.88	.95	92.6
Chauffeur	.60	.71	84.5
Coppersmith	.85	.96	88.5
Machinist	.82	.90	91.1
Diver	1.90	1.90	100.0
Electrician	.90	.95	94.7
Engineman	.81	.88	92.0
Gardener	.63	.63	100.0
Joiner	.85	.92	92.4
Mason, Brick or Stone	1.14	1.14	100.0
Painter	.81	.90	90.0
Welder, Gas	.83	.88	94.3
Pipe Fitter	.90	.94	95.7
Welder, Electric	.83	.89	93.2
Plasterer	1.14	1.14	100.0
Plumber	.90	.94	95.7
Rigger	.81	.90	90.0
Sheet-metal Worker	.89	.95	93.6
Unweighted Average	$ .91	$ .96	94.2

* Source: *Monthly Labor Review*, Feb. 1929, p. 105. The three southern ports are Norfolk, Charleston, and New Orleans. The northern ports are Boston, New York, Philadelphia, Washington, Mare Island, Puget Sound, and Great Lakes.

MISCELLANEOUS EMPLOYMENTS

Practically all of the income and wage data thus far presented apply to persons gainfully employed in agriculture or in manufacturing and mechanical industries. These persons comprise about 65 per cent of the working population of the South. The remaining elements of the population are, however, by no means negligible. According to the Census of Occupations, the ten southern states under consideration had, in 1920, some 643,000 persons gainfully employed in various forms of domestic or personal service. Over half a million of their citizens were employed in trade and about 407,000 of them in transportation. Various kinds of professional service engaged the activity of about 254,000 persons, while over 236,000 were reported as employed in clerical occupations.

A study of income and wages in the South which fails to present at least a modicum of data relative to the important classes enumerated above can scarcely make much claim to completeness. It is unfortunately true, nevertheless, that very little information of the kind desired is available. The Interstate Commerce Commission supplies considerable material bearing on the earnings and wage rates of railroad employees. The Census of Manufactures makes it possible to arrive at an approximate estimate of the average annual salaries of clerks in manufacturing establishments. The United States Bureau of Education compiles detailed statistics relative to the average salaries of public school teachers. Certain private agencies have collected data on the average salaries of ministers and university professors and on the rates of pay of employees in gas and electric plants. This, however, practically exhausts the field of readily obtainable information.

RAILWAY AND PUBLIC UTILITY WAGES

Table XIV compares the average earnings and rates of pay of southern railway and public utility employees with the general level of earnings and wage rates in similar employments elsewhere. It will be noted that the average earnings of southern railroad workers are about 88 per cent of the average earnings in other parts of the country. The wage differential, in other words, appears to approximate

TABLE XIV

Average Earnings and Rates of Pay of Railroad and Public Utility Employees

Item	The South[1]	Outside of the South	Percentage South is of Rest of Country
Average Annual Earnings, All Employees, Class I Railroads, 1927[2]	$1,500.00	$1,710.00	87.7
Average Annual Earnings, Employees in Railroad Repair Shops, 1927[3]	1,376.00	1,537.00	89.5
Average Hourly Rates of Pay, Section Men, Maintenance of Way and Structures, 1928[4]	.33	.41	80.7
Average Hourly Earnings, Employees in Gas Plants, July, 1925[5]	.49	.55	88.9
Average Hourly Earnings, Employees in Electric Plants, July 1925[5]	.48	.62	77.2

[1] For the purpose of the present table it has been necessary to adopt a flexible definition of the term "South." The original definition applies only in the case of employees in railroad repair shops. As regards other railroad employees, the term South means the Southern Region as set up by the Interstate Commerce Commission. Arkansas, Lousiana, and a large part of Virginia are thus dropped, while the state of Kentucky is added. In the case of employees in gas and electric plants, the term South includes not only the ten states selected at the outset of the study but in addition Delaware, Maryland, Kentucky, Oklahoma, Texas, and West Virginia.

[2] Source: Interstate Commerce Commission, *Statistics of Railways in the United States.* Average annual earnings obtained by dividing total compensation of employees by average number employed.

[3] Source: *Census of Manufactures,* 1927. Total wages divided by average number of wage earners.

[4] Source: Interstate Commerce Commission, *Comparative Statement of Operating Averages,* Class I, Steam Railroads in the United States, Years 1925-1928.

[5] Source: National Industrial Conference Board, *Wages in the United States,* p. 66. The report in question gives average hourly earnings by geographic divisions. The figures for average earnings outside of the South, as shown in Table XIV, represent unweighted averages of the appropriate divisional averages.

very closely the differential observed in the case of trade unionists. Inasmuch as railroad workers represent for the most part a body of highly skilled and experienced employees, this is about what might be expected. As might be expected, also, the wage differentials applicable to employees of gas and electric plants are not materially out of line with the differential for railroad employees.

SALARIES OF TEACHERS AND CLERGYMEN

Table XV shows how the annual salaries of southern teachers, college professors, clergymen, and factory clerks compare with the average salaries received in similar callings in other parts of the country. In comparing the salaries of public school teachers, only cities of 10,000 to 30,000 population were considered. This was done advisedly to increase the comparability of the averages. The comparison is still somewhat vitiated by virtue of the fact that it was not possible to eliminate the salaries of Negro teachers in computing the southern average. Data covering six southern states indicate that the average salary of white teachers is about 16 per cent higher than the combined average of white and Negro teachers. If this percentage holds good for all of the ten states under consideration, the average salary of southern white teachers becomes 77 per cent of the average for the rest of the country instead of 68 per cent as indicated in Table XV. But even with this adjustment, it will be seen that the salaries of southern school teachers fall short of the level prevailing elsewhere by a considerably greater percentage than in the parallel case of southern college and university professors, whose salaries average around 88 per cent of the general average for the rest of the country.

TABLE XV

Average Annual Earnings in Specified Professional and Clerical Pursuits.

Occupation	The South[1]	Remainder of Country	Percentage South is of Remainder of Country
Average Annual Salaries of Public School Teachers in Cities of 10,000 to 30,000 Population, 1925-1926[2]	$1,014.	$1,500.	67.6
Average Annual Salaries of College and University Professors, 1926-27[3]	2,660.	3,033.	87.7
Average Annual Salaries of Clergymen, 1920[4]	716.	981.	73.0
Estimated Average Annual Salaries of Male Clerks in Manufacturing Establishments, 1919[5]	1,537.	1,688.	91.0

[1] As regards college and university professors, the term "South" includes the District of Columbia and the states of Delaware, Kentucky, Maryland, Oklahoma, Texas, and West Virginia, in addition to the ten states originally selected.

[2] Source: United States Bureau of Education, *Biennial Survey of Education*, 1924-26, p. 742. Includes salaries of kindergarten, elementary, and high school teachers.

[3] Source: Publications of The General Education Board, *Occasional Papers, No. 8*, Table I, p. 44.

[4] Source: Interchurch World Movement, *World Survey-American Volume*, p. 286.

[5] Source: *Census of Manufactures*, 1919. The averages shown above were obtained by dividing the aggregate of salaries paid by the equated number of clerks. For this purpose one male was considered the equivalent of 1.9 females. For the justification of this procedure see Leven, *Income in the Various States*, pp. 79-80.

This difference is understandable when it is considered that professors are normally drawn from a nation-wide area, whereas public school teachers are as a rule recruited locally.

It will be seen from Table XV that the salaries of southern clergymen average around 73 per cent of the prevailing level elsewhere. This percentage may possibly misrepresent the present situation since it is based on data which are ten years old. It is known, however, that ministers' salaries vary closely with teachers' salaries in different parts of the country.[1] Since the respective salary differentials for teachers and clergymen as given in Table XV are not far apart,

[1] Leven, *Income in the Various States*, p. 95.

it may be assumed that the relative difference in present ministerial salaries, as between the South and elsewhere, is still substantially as indicated.

According to Table XV the average salary of male clerks in southern manufacturing establishments is only nine per cent below the comparable average for the rest of the country. A number of considerations, however, serve to cast doubt upon this result. The figures used are over ten years old and apply to a year in which conditions were abnormal. The salary averages have been estimated on a basis which involved certain questionable assumptions. Finally, in view of the smaller average size of southern establishments, there is no certainty that comparable groups of employees were involved.

OMITTED OCCUPATIONS

In concluding the present survey of southern income and wages, it is pertinent to observe that the picture drawn is far from complete. Important elements of the working population, for instance the large group of domestic servants and the numerous class of persons engaged in trade, have been left out of the reckoning altogether. This deficiency, however, may not be as serious as it appears. The investigations of the National Bureau of Economic Research indicate that wages in occupational groups which are recruited from the same class of society are to a certain extent interdependent.[2] To the degree that this tendency may be relied upon, it is thus possible to consider the wage differentials worked out in the present study for a limited number of employments as representative of the average differentials

[2] Leven, *Income in the Various States*, p. 95.

applying to groups of occupations drawing employees from the same economic class. Making a practical application of this reasoning, it is probably safe to assume that the average wages of southern domestic workers fall short of the prevailing level of wages elsewhere by about the same margin as was noted in the case of unskilled common labor, that is, by from 40 to 50 per cent. The income differential applying to persons engaged in trade is probably considerably less than this. Trade, however, is a general term which encompasses a wide variety of occupations, ranging all the way from newsboys and porters to proprietors of stores and bank presidents. This miscellaneous assortment of employments would obviously have to be broken up into subgroups before any generalizations could be hazarded.

SUMMARY OF FINDINGS

It can scarcely be claimed for the statistical investigation, which has just been brought to a close, that it has resulted in the discovery of any new and startling information. The statistics which have been presented merely supply quantitative confirmation of certain facts and tendencies of which informed Southerners have been aware for a long time. These facts and tendencies may be summarized briefly as follows:

Money incomes and money wages are quite generally lower in the South than in the rest of the country. The degree of difference, however, cannot be summed up in a single percentage which applies uniformly to all industries and types of employment. Notwithstanding the publicity which has lately centered around the lower level of factory earnings, it is not in manufacturing but in agriculture that the income differential between the South and the rest of the country reaches its maximum. This is all the more serious for the South, since agriculture represents the main source of livelihood of nearly half of its population.

The average per capita income of the southern agricultural classes is, roughly speaking, about one-half of the average income received by similar classes in other parts of the country. Outside of agriculture, the extent to which southern earnings and rates of pay fall below those of the rest of the country seems to depend largely on the factor of skill. The differential in rates of pay for the least skilled type of common labor appears to be on a par with the differential in agriculture. For common labor in general, southern wages seem to range from 50 to 65 per cent of the wages in comparable employments elsewhere. In semi-skilled employments, the range of southern wages seems to be from 65 to 85 per cent of the comparable wages paid elsewhere. In the case of skilled mechanics, the disparity between the South and the rest of the country appears to reach its minimum, southern wage rates representing from 75 to 100 per cent of the corresponding wage rates obtaining outside of the South. The differentials noted do not seem to be materially affected by the character of the employing agency, applying in substantially equal degree to wages paid by strictly private enterprises, public utilities, and governments.

The extent to which average wages for entire industries in the South fall short of average wages in similar industries elsewhere is determined largely by the relative proportions of skilled and unskilled workers employed. In industries which employ a high percentage of unskilled workers, as for instance in the sawmill industry, the disparity in wage levels as between the South and the rest of the country is large. In the foundry and machine shop industry, which employs a high percentage of skilled workers, the disparity between the South and the rest of the country is relatively small.

LABOR COSTS AND REAL WAGES

In order to guard against the drawing of unwarranted conclusions, it is important that the limitations of the statistics presented be clearly understood. In the first place, it should be borne in mind that the incomes and wages dealt with are primarily money incomes and money wages. Practically the only gainful activity in which income items other than cash have been taken into account is agriculture.

This particular limitation has very little significance, since most gainfully employed persons other than farmers receive their income in the form of cash. But one exception of some consequence deserves to be noted. Southern textile employees customarily receive certain valuable perquisites in addition to their cash wages. Thus the great majority of them live in company-owned houses for which they pay less than a full commercial rental. Electricity, coal, and wood are also frequently supplied by the companies at less than the full commercial rates. The National Industrial Conference Board estimated the annual value of perquisites such as these at $87 per family in Charlotte, North Carolina, in 1920.[8] No comprehensive statistics on the value of the noncash elements of the average textile worker's income are available, however, and in the present study only money

[8] National Industrial Conference Board, *Special Report No. 8*, May, 1920, p. 18.

wages have been considered. Had it been possible to include the non-cash items, the wage differentials between the South and elsewhere, as regards the textile industry at least, would have been somewhat reduced.

From the point of view of the industrial enterpriser, regional differences in money wages are, of course, not important unless they reflect actual differences in the labor cost of producing comparable commodities. In other words, the employer of labor is interested not only in the money wage which he pays out but in the value of the services which the worker gives in return for his wages. Low money wages do not necessarily mean low labor costs. It would be a serious mistake, therefore, to assume that the differences in money wages between the South and the rest of the country, as worked out for the present purpose, represent corresponding differences in labor costs per unit of product. The spread of industry to the South in recent years, coupled with the known differentials in money wages, make it a reasonable supposition that southern labor costs, in certain productive activities at least, are somewhat lower than elsewhere. However, the statistics on money wages developed in the present study are not of themselves sufficient to prove the correctness of this supposition.

Just as the employer of labor is interested primarily in labor costs, so the wage receiver is interested not so much in his money wages as in his real wages, that is, in the standard of living which his money wages will enable him to support in the particular locality in which he lives. It would doubtless be desirable to know to what extent the differences in money incomes worked out for the present study correspond to differences in real incomes. This information might not be difficult to obtain, if the living requirements and tastes of wage earners were everywhere alike and if there were no qualitative but only quantitative differences in real incomes. But as a matter of actual fact, such variables as climate and other environmental factors, as well as dissimilarities in social habits, render any attempt to measure the disparity in real income as between the South and elsewhere an extremely hazardous undertaking.

The fact that the income and wage differentials given in the present study have not been adjusted for regional differences in the cost of living does not deprive these figures of their primary significance. As has already been indicated, the average amount of money income per capita in the South is less than half of the corresponding average for the rest of the country. So great a disparity in money income must necessarily carry with it a significant difference in real income in a country as closely integrated, economically, as is the United States, in which a large proportion of the necessities and satisfactions of life are supplied by organizations which operate on a national scale.

A consideration of even greater importance from the standpoint of the present investigation is the fact that the translation of money wages into real wages would not change the relative size of the various wage differentials with reference to one another. In other words, the measurement of wages in terms of commodities and services instead of in terms of money would not affect the relationship observed to exist between the size of the wage differential and the factor of occupational skill.

CHAPTER V

WHY SOUTHERN INCOMES ARE LOW

THE FACTS of the southern income and wage situation, as they have just been summarized, raise one or two questions which invite further discussion. In the first place, what factors are responsible for the South's extremely low average of income per capita? According to the figures of the National Bureau of Economic Research, shown in Table II, the total income of the South divided by the total population yields a quotient which on the average is less than half as great as the corresponding quotient for the rest of the country. These figures, it is true, refer to the years 1919, 1920, and 1921. However, as indicated by the data contained in Tables III and IV, in neither agriculture nor manufacturing have subsequent changes been great enough to make the present relative position of the South materially different.

One circumstance which partially accounts for the South's low average is the relatively small number of Southerners belonging to the higher income classes. This factor cannot be rated as of prime importance, since the recipients of very large incomes are not sufficiently numerous nor sufficiently affluent to exercise a marked influence on the general income average.[1] Another factor, of course, is the lower scale of wages and salaries in the South, as well as the smaller returns per worker in agriculture. This, however, does not offer a complete explanation. As has been noted, the average amount of income per capita in the South

[1] See King, *The National Income and Its Purchasing Power*, p. 178.

is less than half of the corresponding average for the rest of the country. Not even in agriculture nor in the least skilled of non-agricultural employments are the disparities in per capita productivity and rates of pay as great as the disparity in per capita income. It is obvious that another factor must be looked for in order to explain adequately the low average of income in the South. That factor is found in the occupational distribution of its population.

The rewards offered by the various forms of gainful employment are by no means all alike. Manufacturing yields a larger average return per person engaged in it than does agriculture. Some forms of manufacturing activity yield larger returns per worker than do others. Irrespective of regional differences in wage and salary scales, it is possible for one geographic area to have a lower average level of income than another simply because its working population is more highly concentrated in occupations and employments of relatively low return. This is one of the main reasons for the low level of income in the South. A disproportionately high percentage of its population is employed in the low-yield industries.

THE PREPONDERANCE OF LOW-YIELD OCCUPATIONS

Under present conditions, agriculture probably offers smaller returns to those engaging in it than any other major economic activity. The per capita productivity of southern agriculture, as has been seen, is particularly low. Nevertheless about 46 per cent of the southern population depends on agriculture for support. Elsewhere, the proportion of the population which still elects to support itself by farming is only 24 per cent.

Since manufacturing on the whole yields larger per worker returns than does agriculture, a shift of man power from the latter to the former activity would tend to increase the South's per capita income. During recent years, the number of factory wage earners in southern establishments has been increasing steadily. The percentage of the southern population engaged in manufacturing and mechanical pursuits, however, is still far below the average for the rest of the country.[2] Moreover, the particular industries which employ the largest number of southern workers are, generally speaking, industries which rely heavily on unskilled and semi-skilled labor and in which average earnings per worker are consequently low. This fact is brought out by Table XVI, which shows the relative importance of specific types of manufacturing activity in the South from the point of view of the number of wage earners employed.

It will be noted from Table XVI that half of the industrial wage earners of the South are concentrated in two industries, textiles and lumber and timber. Regardless of where they are carried on, both of these industries rank low as regards average earnings per worker employed. Massachusetts employs more cotton textile workers than any other state outside of the South. The average annual earnings of its textile workers, as indicated by the Census of Manufactures, fell short of the average earnings of other factory wage earners within the state by approximately 24 per cent in 1927. In Michigan, the average annual earnings of workers in the lumber and timber industry were some 27 per cent

[2] In 1920, according to the *Census of Occupations,* 18.1 per cent of the working population of the South was engaged in manufacturing and mechanical pursuits as compared with 33.7 per cent of the working population elsewhere.

below the general average of other industrial wage earners within the state. Even in Oregon, where wages in the lumber and timber industry are exceptionally high, there was, nevertheless, a disparity of nine per cent between the average earnings of workers in that industry and the general average of earnings applicable to other industries of the state, in 1927.

In most of the northern industrial states, the effect of the low-wage industries is more or less offset by the presence of industries in which earnings per worker are high. Notable examples of high high-wage industries are printing and

TABLE XVI

Number of Wage Earners Employed in Specific Types of Manufacturing Activity in the South, Year 1927.*

Type of Activity	Average Number of Wage Earners Employed	Percentage of Total
Textiles:		
Cotton Goods	$270,995	25.8
Knit Goods	47,063	4.5
TOTAL	$318,058	30.3
Lumber and Timber Products:		
Planing mill products	21,951	2.1
Lumber and timber products not elsewhere classified	193,155	18.4
TOTAL	$215,106	20.5
Railroad Repair Shops	59,800	5.7
Tobacco and Tobacco Products	36,971	3.5
Turpentine and Rosin	33,766	3.2
Furniture	28,356	2.7
Iron and Steel Products Including Cast Iron Pipe	24,009	2.3
All Others	335,898	31.8
GRAND TOTAL	$1,051,964	100.0

*_Census of Manufactures_, 1927.

publishing, automobiles, iron and steel, and foundry and machine shop products. These industries are either absent altogether from the South or are very weakly represented.

The foregoing considerations make it evident that the low average of income per capita in the South is due in the main to three factors: (1) the relatively small number of persons receiving large incomes; (2) the lower scale of salaries and wages coupled with the small return per worker in southern agriculture; (3) the concentration of the working population in industries and employments which yield a relatively low return per worker no matter where they are carried on.

INDUSTRIAL WAGES AND AGRICULTURAL PRODUCTIVITY

In order completely to explain the difference in per capita income as between the South and elsewhere, it is necessary to account for the wage and salary differentials which were observed to be present in varying degree in practically all of the occupations studied. To treat this subject in any basic fashion would carry the discussion far afield. A complex of many interrelated factors, not all of them economic, is doubtless involved. The immobility of certain elements of the southern working population and the presence of the Negro with his low standard of living and limited range of occupational choices are obvious elements to be considered. It is not proposed here to go behind the statistical data which have just been presented. These data point to a strong relationship between the depressed level of southern wages and the low income-yielding capacity of southern agriculture.

It has been observed that the income differential between

the South and the rest of the country is greater in the case of agriculture than in the case of any other employment considered. It is in this submerged industry that nearly half of the southern population gains its livelihood. In view of these considerations, it is highly significant that it is in the unskilled occupations capable of being filled by raw recruits from the farm that the wage differential between the South and the rest of the country reaches its maximum. In semiskilled occupations, which are less immediately affected by the competition of the agricultural classes, the wage differential is considerably diminished. Finally, in highly skilled occupations, which are for the most part out of reach of potential industrial workers from the farm, the wage differential is at a minimum and in some cases entirely disappears.

FARMERS' INCOMES

There is abundant evidence that the annual incomes of hundreds of thousands of farmers in the South are so depressed that employment in manufacturing establishments even at existing southern wages would constitute for them a decided advance in the economic scale. Although there are no comprehensive statistics on the average incomes received by farmers in different sections of the country, the Department of Agriculture collects annually certain sample data from which important conclusions may be drawn. The department has compiled detailed returns covering the operations in 1927 of 5,255 southern farms.[3] The average net

[3] *Yearbook of Agriculture,* 1928, p. 1038. The statistics used cover farms located in the South Atlantic and South Central States. That is, the territory covered includes in addition to the ten states selected for the present study, the states of Delaware, Maryland, West Virginia, Kentucky, Texas, and Oklahoma.

income from these farms, including the value of food produced and used on the farm, and after the deduction of interest at 5 per cent on the farm investment, was $635 in the South Atlantic States and $700 in the South Central States. These figures represent family incomes, since the value of labor contributed by members of the farmers' family has not been deducted.

Low as the income figures in question may appear, there are strong reasons for believing that they present too optimistic a picture to be truly representative of the conditions prevailing among the rank and file of southern farmers. The average size of southern farms is less than 80 acres. The farms from which returns were received by the Department of Agriculture averaged 189 acres in the South Atlantic States and 249 acres in the South Central States. The farms in question, moreover, were owner-operated farms. Of the 2,060,000 farms reported by the 1925 Census of Agriculture in the ten southern states which form the basis of the present study, only 47 per cent were operated by owners or managers. The remaining 53 per cent represented tenant-operated farms. About 516,000 of the tenant operators, or slightly less than half of them, were so-called croppers, that is, married laborers, without capital of their own, hired to raise a crop for a half interest.

There can be no doubt that the average income of all southern farmers, including the 1,090,000 tenant farmers, is considerably lower than indicated by the farm returns received by the Department of Agriculture. It is possible to arrive at a rough approximation of the true average on the basis of the figures for gross farm income given in Table B on page 19. As indicated in that table, the gross value of all farm products, with duplications eliminated, amounted to about $2,139,000,000 in the ten states under consideration in 1927. Dividing this amount among the 2,060,000 farms gives a gross income per farm of $1,038. In the case of the 5,255 southern farms, for which detailed cost statistics were collected by the Department of Agriculture, the net return to the farmer, including the value of farm products consumed by his family, and after the deduction of interest at five per cent on the farm investment, represented approximately 50 per cent of the gross farm income. If this percentage may be taken as applying generally, the conclusion follows that the average southern farmer received a net return for his labor and managerial functions of approximately $519 in 1927.

FARM AND INDUSTRIAL INCOMES COMPARED

Although the two sets of figures are not, strictly speaking, comparable, it is worth while to contrast the average farmer's income, as calculated above, with the average annual earnings of southern factory workers, as indicated by the 1927 Census of Manufactures. The census average wage, obtained by dividing the annual factory wage bill by the average number of workers employed, represents an individual and not a family income. It is an average, moreover, which has been diluted by the inclusion of women and minors. In view of these facts, it is all the more significant that in the same year in which southern farmers had an average income of only $519 per capita, southern factory workers, taken as a whole, had average annual earnings of $823 per capita; the average annual earnings of workers in the lumber and timber industry amounted to $748; while, in the cotton goods industry, earnings per worker averaged around $671 per annum.

It would, of course, be a mistake to assume that all southern farmers receive an income equal to $519 per year as a reward for their agricultural efforts. That great numbers receive considerably less than this is indicated by a study made by the North Carolina Tax Commission covering the operations of 1,115 North Carolina farms in 1927. The poorest farms studied were located in the mountain counties of the western portion of the state. Returns from 281 sample farms located in three of these mountain counties indicated an average cash income per farm of $86. Including income received in kind, and without deduction of interest on the farm investment, the average income was $554 per farm. Deduction of interest at five per cent on the value of the farm investment left an average of only $273 as the farmer's labor and managerial income.[4] In the same year, 1927, workers in North Carolina cotton mills had an average census wage of $694 per annum.

FUTURE OF THE WAGE DIFFERENTIAL

To the theoretically minded, the South today presents the spectacle of an economic system in unstable equilibrium. Southern wage rates, especially for unskilled labor, are considerably below the average for the rest of the country. Manufacturing offers larger rewards to the rank and file of southern workers than are normally obtainable in agriculture. Theoretically, this situation should be expected to set strong currents in motion. Industrial enterprises, whose successful

[4] *Report of the North Carolina Tax Commission, 1928*, p. 119.

operation depends upon the availability of large numbers of unskilled and semi-skilled employees, should be expected to move to the South. There should be a flow of labor from agriculture to manufacturing, a flow which should be comparatively rapid in view of the South's million or more tenant farmers with little in the way of capital investment to tie them to the land. There should also be some tendency for southern labor to migrate to the high wage industrial centers of the North.

Such scant statistical evidence as is available indicates that the movements described have to a certain extent actually been taking place. Manufacturing activity in the South has been expanding more rapidly than in the rest of the country. According to the Census of Manufactures, the number of factory wage earners employed outside of the South decreased by about nine per cent between 1919 and 1927. Within the South, however, the number of persons employed in manufacturing establishments increased by nine per cent during the same period. Although the shift of man power from agriculture to other employments is not peculiar to any particular region, the movement seems to be progressing more rapidly in the South than elsewhere. Thus, between 1920 and 1925, the farm population of the ten southern states under consideration showed a decline of approximately 12 per cent. Outside of the South the decline in the farm population was only six per cent.[5] The

[5] The farm population figures for 1925 are not strictly comparable with those reported in 1920, since the definition used in 1920 included not only persons living on farms, but, in addition, farm laborers and their families who, while not living on farms, did live in rural territory. The Census Bureau expresses the belief that the number of laborers thus included is not very great.

absolute decline in the southern farm population between 1920 and 1925 was in the neighborhood of 1,300,000 persons. Some part, at least, of this loss was due to migration to the North as is evidenced by the rapid growth of the Negro population of certain northern cities.

An optimist might be inclined to view the tendencies noted above as an augury of the ultimate disappearance of the southern wage differential. He would doubtless seek to justify his faith by reasoning somewhat as follows:

Wages in the South are low because the sole source of livelihood of nearly half of the population is a particularly unprofitable agriculture. If agriculture could be made to yield a more adequate living to the present masses of southern farm dwellers, there would be a corresponding rise in the level of industrial wages. If such a solution be regarded as chimerical, the only other alternative, aside from migration, is to create opportunities for employment in more remunerative lines of endeavor. Even at the present scale of wages, industry has more to offer the southern worker than has agriculture. If industry can be expanded to the point where it is capable of absorbing the sub-marginal workers on the farms, the wage differential between the South and the rest of the country should, in the course of time, automatically disappear. Pending the completion of this process, the wage differential has a useful purpose, for it serves both as a lure to attract the industrial capitalist and as a stimulus to migration. To attempt to reduce or remove it by artificial means would only retard the growth of southern industry and condemn the tenant farmer to a longer period of poverty on his farm.

Individuals who have less faith than the optimist in the beneficent workings of unregulated economic forces are not likely to find this reasoning convincing. They may very well point out that the income disparity between the South and the rest of the country is as old at least as the Civil War and that it has not as yet disappeared automatically. In the opinion of such as these, the present situation in the South calls for a high order of economic statesmanship rather than for a supine policy of *laissez-faire*.

If the latter view is correct, and if more positive measures are required to raise the level of income in the South, one fact seems clear. Such measures, if they are to succeed, must not neglect the South's two million farmers.

www.ingramcontent.com/pod-product-compliance
Lightning Source LLC
LaVergne TN
LVHW090429210926
848480LV00002B/748
* 9 7 8 1 4 6 9 6 4 4 5 8 5 *